Animals That Live in the Desert / Animales del desierto

Gila Monsters/ Monstruos de Gila

JoAnn Early Macken

Reading consultant/Consultora de lectura:
Susan Nations, M. Ed., author, literacy coach,
consultant/autora, tutora de alfabetización, consultora

WEEKLY READER
EARLY LEARNING LIBRARY

Please visit our web site at: www.earlyliteracy.cc
For a free color catalog describing Weekly Reader® Early Learning Library's list
of high-quality books, call 1-877-445-5824 (USA) or 1-800-387-3178 (Canada).
Weekly Reader® Early Learning Library's fax: (414) 336-0164.

Library of Congress Cataloging-in-Publication Data available upon request from publisher.
Fax (414) 336-0157 for the attention of the Publishing Records Department.

ISBN 0-8368-4841-1 (lib. bdg.)
ISBN 0-8368-4848-9 (softcover)

This edition first published in 2006 by
Weekly Reader® Early Learning Library
A Member of the WRC Media Family of Companies
330 West Olive Street, Suite 100
Milwaukee, WI 53212 USA

Art direction: Tammy West
Cover design and page layout: Kami Koenig
Picture research: Diane Laska-Swanke
Translators: Tatiana Acosta and Guillermo Gutiérrez

Picture credits: Cover, © Mary McDonald/Visuals Unlimited; pp. 5, 9, 21 © John
Cancalosi/naturepl.com; p. 7 © Jeff Foott/naturepl.com; p. 11 © Joe McDonald/
Visuals Unlimited; p. 13 © Lynn M. Stone; pp. 15, 17, 19 © Jim Merli/Visuals Unlimited

Printed in the United States of America

1 2 3 4 5 6 7 8 9 09 08 07 06 05

Note to Educators and Parents

Reading is such an exciting adventure for young children! They are beginning to integrate their oral language skills with written language. To encourage children along the path to early literacy, books must be colorful, engaging, and interesting; they should invite the young reader to explore both the print and the pictures.

Animals That Live in the Desert is a new series designed to help children read about creatures that make their homes in dry places. Each book explains where a different desert animal lives, what it eats, and how it adapts to its arid environment.

Each book is specially designed to support the young reader in the reading process. The familiar topics are appealing to young children and invite them to read — and reread — again and again. The full-color photographs and enhanced text further support the student during the reading process.

In addition to serving as wonderful picture books in schools, libraries, homes, and other places where children learn to love reading, these books are specifically intended to be read within an instructional guided reading group. This small group setting allows beginning readers to work with a fluent adult model as they make meaning from the text. After children develop fluency with the text and content, the book can be read independently. Children and adults alike will find these books supportive, engaging, and fun!

— Susan Nations, M.Ed., author, literacy coach,
and consultant in literacy development

Nota para los maestros y los padres

¡Leer es una aventura tan emocionante para los niños pequeños! A esta edad están comenzando a integrar su manejo del lenguaje oral con el lenguaje escrito. Para animar a los niños en el camino de la lectura incipiente, los libros deben ser coloridos, estimulantes e interesantes; deben invitar a los jóvenes lectores a explorar la letra impresa y las ilustraciones.

Animales del desierto es una nueva colección diseñada para que los niños lean textos sobre animales que viven en lugares muy secos. Cada libro explica dónde vive un animal del desierto, qué come y cómo se adapta a su árido medio ambiente.

Cada libro está especialmente diseñado para ayudar a los jóvenes lectores en el proceso de lectura. Los temas familiares llaman la atención de los niños y los invitan a leer —y releer— una y otra vez. Las fotografías a todo color y el tamaño de la letra ayudan aún más al estudiante en el proceso de lectura.

Además de servir como maravillosos libros ilustrados en escuelas, bibliotecas, hogares y otros lugares donde los niños aprenden a amar la lectura, estos libros han sido especialmente concebidos para ser leídos en un grupo de lectura guiada. Este contexto permite que los lectores incipientes trabajen con un adulto que domina la lectura mientras van determinando el significado del texto. Una vez que los niños dominan el texto y el contenido, el libro puede ser leído de manera independiente. ¡Estos libros les resultarán útiles, estimulantes y divertidos a niños y a adultos por igual!

— Susan Nations, M.Ed., autora/tutora de alfabetización/
consultora de desarrollo de la lectura

The Gila (HEEL-ah) monster is a lizard. It is the largest lizard that lives in the United States. Its bite has **venom**, or poison.

El monstruo de Gila es un lagarto. Es el lagarto más grande de Estados Unidos. Su mordedura es **venenosa**.

Lizards are reptiles. They move
into the sun to warm up. They
hide in the shade to stay cool.

▬ ▬ ▬ ▬ ▬ ▬ ▬ ▬ ▬ ▬ ▬ ▬ ▬ ▬ ▬

Los lagartos son reptiles. Se
ponen al sol para calentarse.
Se esconden en la sombra
para refrescarse.

Gila monsters live in the desert. They hide most of the time. In the winter, they **hibernate**, or sleep. In the summer, they rest under the ground.

Los monstruos de Gila viven en el desierto. La mayor parte del tiempo están escondidos. En el invierno **hibernan**, es decir, duermen. En el verano, descansan bajo tierra.

The Gila monster is covered with scales. The scales look like beads. Some are black. Some are pink or orange.

El monstruo de Gila está cubierto de escamas. Las escamas parecen bolitas. Algunas son negras. Otras son rosadas o anaranjadas.

scales/
escamas

11

The Gila monster has strong claws. Its teeth are sharp. Its forked tongue is purple.

El monstruo de Gila tiene fuertes garras. Sus dientes son afilados. Su lengua bífida es de color morado.

claws/
garras

tongue/
lengua

13

Gila monsters eat eggs. They eat eggs from birds, snakes, and turtles. They eat small animals and birds.

- - - - - - - - - - - - - - - -

Los monstruos de Gila comen huevos. Se comen los huevos de pájaros, serpientes y tortugas. También comen animales pequeños y pájaros.

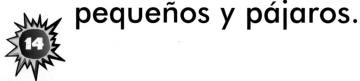

A Gila monster can eat a huge meal. It may not eat again for a long time. It stores fat in its tail. Later, it lives on the fat.

———————————————————

Un monstruo de Gila puede comer mucho de una vez. Luego es capaz de no volver a comer en mucho tiempo. Almacena la grasa en su cola. Luego, vive de esa grasa.

tail/
cola

17

Female Gila monsters lay eggs in the sand. The eggs stay warm in the sun. Babies hatch from the eggs. The babies have teeth and venom.

- - - - - - - - - - - - - - - -

Las hembras ponen sus huevos en la arena. Los huevos se calientan con el sol. Las crías salen de los huevos. Las crías tienen dientes y veneno.

eggs/
huevos

19

If a Gila monster is scared, it tries to back away. It may even open its mouth and hiss. If it cannot escape, it may bite!

Si un monstruo de Gila se asusta, tratará de huir. Podría también abrir la boca y emitir un sonido sibilante. Si no consigue escapar, ¡puede morder!

GLOSSARY

desert — a very dry place

forked — split or divided

lizard — a reptile with scaly skin, four legs, and a long, thin body and tail

reptiles — cold-blooded animals with bones and scales. Snakes, lizards, and turtles are reptiles.

scales — thin, flat plates that cover the bodies of snakes, fish, and other animals

GLOSARIO

bífida — separada o dividida

desierto — un lugar muy seco

escamas — placas delgadas y planas que cubren el cuerpo de las serpientes, los peces y otros animales

lagarto — reptil con piel escamosa, cuatro patas, cuerpo largo y fino y cola

reptiles — animales de sangre fría, huesos y escamas. Las serpientes, los lagartos y las tortugas son reptiles.

FOR MORE INFORMATION/ MÁS INFORMACIÓN

BOOKS IN ENGLISH

The Gila Monster. Lizard Library (series). Jake Miller (PowerKids Press)

Way Out in the Desert. T. J. Marsh and Jennnifer Ward (Rising Moon Books)

LIBROS EN ESPAÑOL

El autobús mágico se reseca: un libro sobre los desiertos. Suzanne Weyn (Scholastic)

Listen to the Desert/Oye al desierto. Pat Mora (Clarion)

INDEX

ÍNDICE

ABOUT THE AUTHOR

JoAnn Early Macken is the author of two rhyming picture books, *Sing-Along Song* and *Cats on Judy*, and many other nonfiction books for beginning readers. Her poems have appeared in several children's magazines. A graduate of the M.F.A. in Writing for Children and Young Adults program at Vermont College, she lives in Wisconsin with her husband and their two sons. Visit her Web site at www.joannmacken.com.

INFORMACIÓN SOBRE LA AUTORA

JoAnn Early Macken ha escrito dos libros de rimas con ilustraciones, *Sing-Along Song y Cats on Judy*, y muchos otros libros de no ficción para lectores incipientes. Sus poemas han sido publicados en varias revistas infantiles. JoAnn se graduó en el programa M.F.A. de Escritura para Niños y Jóvenes de Vermont College. Vive en Wisconsin con su esposo y sus dos hijos. Puedes visitar su página web: www.joannmacken.com